SACRED PRECINCT

SACRED PRECINCT
BY JACQUELINE KUDLER

SIXTEEN RIVERS PRESS
SAN FRANCISCO

Acknowledgments

Thanks are due to the following journals where these poems first appeared:

America's Review: "Amnesty Letters"
Amherst Review: "Out There"
The Artful Mind: "Evening Primrose"
Barnabe Mountain Review: "Amnesty Letters," "The Falling"
Beside the Sleeping Maiden: "Power Outage"
Birmingham Poetry Review: "Persephone"
Convolvulus: "Cherry Pie," "Glass," "Words"
Earth's Daughters: "Hiking with Helen"
Essential Love: "Wedding Day"
Estero: "Alaska," "Instead of Nothing"
Knowing Stones: "The Day We Saw the Elephant"
Marin Poetry Center Anthology I: "Instead of Nothing," "Just,"
    "Sarah," "The Scar"
Other Testaments: "Sarah"
Perihelion: "Words"
Poetry Magazine Online: "And Finally, Amelia Tells It to the Press,"
    "To the Woman Who Will Open This Time Capsule 100 Years from Now"
Poets On: "Lost," "Matters of Survival," "The Scar"
Terminus: A Journal of Literature and Art: "Revelation"
Writing for Our Lives: "First Time," "The House," "My Last Cigarette"

Published by Sixteen Rivers Press
P.O. Box 640663
San Francisco, California 94164-0663
www.sixteenrivers.com

ISBN 0-9707370-4-1
Library of Congress Catalog Card Number 2002-036579

Cover and book design: EudesCo.
Cover art: *The Procession,* by Marilyn Markowitz

For Joel

CONTENTS

≈ *AMNESTY LETTERS*

≈ *OUT THERE*

WORDS

First, of course, *I love you,*
then, the requisite indulgences:
> *You may take two pieces*
>> *You may take a recess*
>>> *You may take three giant steps.*

There are words with indefinite referents:
freedom   beauty   unicorn   God
and words with referents definite beyond dispute
clay   cucumber
unicorn
God.

There are phrases that deliver us from dailiness:
extended   sea   voyage
phrases we seem to wait forever for:
it's a go   it's a boy   it's benign

and if, at the end, words also fail us,
still, there are terms
we'd be hard put
to refuse:
> *after a long, inspired life*
>> *after a brief illness*
>>> *after an extended sea voyage.*

FIRST TIME

Through the first gate,
Into our first world, shall we follow
The deception of the thrush? Into our first world.

—T. S. ELIOT
from *Four Quartets*

GOING HOME

The lobby doors were heavy then,
oak-heavy and dark as coal smoke.
You pushed in hard from an outside
of potsy, box ball, ringelevio into the hollow
inside smells of stone floors, old dust,
tapped the elevator button, rode the groans
and sighs of the aging cable all the way up
to the sixth floor. You didn't need a key then—
she was always home, answering the bell
in her yellow apron, mouth set in its reassuring
crescent of safety and resignation.

             Whatever
is home is always there in the five rooms
redolent with red cabbage simmering in
the sweet-and sour, *Easy Aces* crackling
on the kitchen radio. You throw your jacket
on your bed (despite what she says),
go to the paper dolls already set up on
the window sill, step into the world you make
and make again every afternoon.

FIRST TIME

If it had been about passion—
tide of wild iris cresting,
flesh at rapt attention—

but she had set the time,
the place slowly, mindfully
like setting a table for

dinner: here—they would meet
after class on the steps of Boylan
Hall, here in the elevator cage—

sway of cables impelling them
upward—begin the first embrace,
here in her room, by witness of

the crinoline doll, the one-eyed
bear, finish the thing that had begun
between them that past summer.

If it had been about love, about
the first incursion of the eyes,
the free fall, the final nakedness,

but here—in the middle of a
Monday—he had centered himself
above her life, all fire and

focus, and she, entered, held
him in the circle of her thighs,
for all she knew of love was

what she could not bear to lose.
Yet later when she left him at
the subway stop, strolled home

alone in the beveled light of
late December, the sky between
the buildings seemed wider,

somehow, seemed alive, and
like the space between her legs,
amazing.

PERSEPHONE

By March, I try to remember
brightness, how it moves over
the planes of her face the way
light might play over a field
of grain at harvest, but by March
I've almost forgotten the light too,
so when she comes down to claim me,
arms outstretched, tears letting down
like warm milk all over the plump

curve of her cheeks, and clasps
me to her too-ample breast crying
*Child of my heart, what has he
done with you?* could I tell her

how it was, holding the darkness
close around my shoulders like a
deep fur, his hand all the while
stroking my belly, the inside of
my thigh, could I tell her what it
meant to let my breath go easy, feel
his breathing in the current of my
blood, my appetite opened to more,
oh more, than pomegranate seeds.

NINO

You are in your garden. I see you
dozing there below the gray lace of
olive branches, remains of your
afternoon Strega smouldering
in the glass at your hand. If I listen
long enough I can hear the voices
of your grandchildren fluttering
somewhere among the trellises,
for you are old now too, of course,
age lying benignly on the polished
planes of your face, as youth
did that day you called to me
across the Rialto—*Sabrina,*
you called (1956, the summer of
Audrey Hepburn, and I too was
ponytailed, shirtwaisted in my
new drip-dry), or was it your friend
Franco who called, the one we
had to admit *did* look just like
K-e-e-rk DooGLASS,
and was he calling my friend, Irene,
with her ponytail, shirtwaist, and sloe
eyes, and did you and I end up
together that evening by default
kissing on a bench by a *bacino*
on the Grand Canal, kissing
long and deep. How courtly
you were then, Nino, breathing
Venetian ardor into my ear:
Is it possible, you sighed, *to fall
in love in one night?* (exactly
the words, as it turned out, Franco
breathed to Irene on the bench
opposite). But I remember thinking

whatever I'd come to Venice for
would surely taste like this, and
murmured, *Yes, it must be,* all
the while pushing your hand from
my breast, just one more time.
Oh, you sighed again—centuries
of defeated doges sighing
alongside you, *You are too strong
for me, you American girls.*

JUST

Too small still for
smiles or eyebrows,
her world is bounded
by the breast on the
one hand, dreams
of the breast on the
other.

Fat little finchling
all chirp and feather,
her head lolls wobbly
on my shoulder as I
lay her between us on
the same big bed where
(sweet spasm dazzle
of dark) we made her
father, thirty years
ago.

Turning first one
side, then the other,
she holds us each a
moment in her blue,
diffuse regard, then
floats a flurry of
sucking back inward
toward sleep.

Everything about
her is new. Like
a chiffon shirt just
lifted out from tissue
paper, she smells of
nothing ever worn.

And creaseless,
except the finest
package folds at
neck, wrist,
shoulder.

Just when we'd
begun to notice
a new nest of
wrinkles above
our knees, when
conversation seemed
less succulent, sex
less reliable,
raspberries less
satisfying,

just
when we were
getting good
at seriously
letting
go—
Sasha.

MY LAST CIGARETTE

Last night
of the year,
after love,
light leaking away
from the flesh
so imperceptibly
our bodies blur
at the edges.

Above us,
two black balloons
brush the ceiling,
cords anchored at
the headboard.

Between us,
my paper tiara, tipped
against the pillow,
dusts our sheets,
our cheeks with
silver tinsel.

How fine
to lie beside you,
smoking, pulling pleasure
into my body, steadying
it on top of a breath,
letting it go.

LAST TIMES

I've been thinking about last times,
how some we see happening
like this afternoon in late summer,
your last home.

How gently you set aside what will not travel,
and fold what will to fit the limits
of your new suitcase.

Your father sorts the soccer shoes,
oiling each against its special weather,
rubbing all to a glow, each long slow stroke
a summons.

I layer bread crumbs and apples,
rinds already tasting of autumn,
fixing dessert for dinner, your favorite,
I think, and think about last times

how some we see happening
and some seem to pass unattended
like a last trip to the zoo.

Or, all those years ago,
fingers linked,
walking between the cages,
through smells of dung and spun sugar,
under the insult of the monkeys' eyes,
did we know all along
we were never coming back?

THE HOUSE

The whole house
is waiting—for you
to walk in at your pleasure—
It is yours.

—**WILLIAM CARLOS WILLIAMS**
from "The House"

THE HOUSE

Everywhere she looked, it had taken on
age, a patina of cracks and shadows winter
mornings when the sun slid at a slant under
half-drawn shades, showing more than she
needed to see. They had served each other
well, the house and she—each day she'd
driven dust back to the outer rims of windows,
edges of walls, had shaken out wrinkles from
sheets, teased cobwebs off crossbeams. Each
night the house had curled around them,
clandestine as a cat—all whispers and
wheezes—held them hidden from the absence
of light lurking just the other side of plate
glass doors. The house had held their

sons once, and though she'd thought to
put their rooms to better uses once they'd
gone, she'd failed finally to understand what
such uses might be, so the rooms, denuded of
any claim to their existing lives, remained
as they had been: the balsa biplanes still
suspended from the ceiling, the bust of
Beethoven glowering on the piano...the
metronome. She had not noticed how the
house had taken on weight, how the disused
rooms anchored its western edges and the
steamer trunk with its cache of Halloween
costumes, candy-stripe curtains, held down
the east, how the house had taken on

gravity—and gradually, like a story that
springs some serious subplots, an extra
character too many. Still, it was her
story. She had composed it, knew what was
squirreled away and where, so that nothing
in the house was hidden from her.

It was hers.

THE ROOM AT THE BOTTOM OF MY HOUSE

In the room at the bottom of my house,
I slide an iron over the back of a blue work shirt,
along the sleeve—halved, aligned on its axis from cuff to
shoulder—into the wrist tucks, puddled with rinse water.

In my hand the iron is a climate complete in itself,
its various weathers settling in, sure and sudden as a first frost
flattening furrows, smoothing seams, altering landscapes
according to my whim.

Upstairs, all windows open outward to the sea
but here, where the house leans close into the hillside,
is one small window and the only view
is earthward.

Here, in the room at the bottom of my house
among these smells of soap and pressed denim,
lulled by the intimate mutter of machines,
I slide my iron over the back of a blue work shirt

and watch from my window
a small rain, green and certain,
slide over the stems
right down to the roots of things.

RECITE

For Carolyn

First, a room where everything
is known: the segmented drawers,
high cupboards, cool granite
countertops. Where whatever
is hidden away—sugar in the copper
tin, flour in the red enamel—
waits ready to your hand.

You must not rush here, no, but
set aside the time you'll need—
the lifetime of a long afternoon at least,
preferably a dark one (thrum of rain
on the overhead tile), and the only
light is inside the kitchen.

The madeleine molds must be made
of tin, and ridged like scallop shells—
ingredients tepid to the touch before
you start: flour basking in a warm
oven, ardor of butter-sizzle cooling
over ice water. There'll be no

congealing of hard facts here, but
each discrete texture bending
outward to the altogether new.
Finally, lay out the whisk, the sifter,
take the wooden spoon in hand.
There's nothing left to do now
but begin.

INSTEAD OF NOTHING

...from the very fact that something exists instead of nothing, there is in possible things...a claim to existence.

—G. W. LEIBNIZ
Principles of Nature and of Grace Founded on Reason

The morning the rain came
down in feathered drum riffs
on the bedroom roof, and under
the kitchen eaves   shimmer

and bounce and spreading
circles of   oh   and
three brown birds rocking
on feeder perches, sputter of
yellow leaves on slick black
branches   something

wool socks steaming on heat
vents, wheat toast and apple
tea   a good day to stay
inside, air   everywhere
inlit   extra dimension
of dark   a   good

day to sort last summer's
photos gather wool
jackets from the downstairs
closet,   ponder   quantum
fluctuations,   gutters

running slow

                              slide

of glitter down
glass panes   a good
day
to do (instead of)
nothing.

POWER OUTAGE

Once you've seen mud
move, whole hillsides
shimmy, slip seaward,
once you've heard
earth give, settle,
make its own small
corrections, you know
how tenuous any toe-
hold here can be.

Once you've seen
love fall away,
vanish in a bandaged
word, a clattering
silence, you lose all
disposition toward
long views, hold
tight to the near
at hand. All day

long, while rain
lapped posts below
our floor boards,
toppled power poles
above, I simmered
Taki's chicken soup
over a low gas
flame. Tonight,

together, we sit
down by candlelight
to sip the hot of it
from steaming bowls,
along with crusty
bread, arugula, and
good Greek wine.

EVENING PRIMROSE

For Joel

All fall, it lingers in the empty
basil bed, hangs in through winter too.
Come March, I dream about my green
seedlings, already redolent of Genoa.
About *pesto, pasta verde, zuppa di funghi.*
Then I think about the dailiness of you
and what endures...and let the weed be.
And tend it, of course, right out under the
kitchen window, where things grow savory
instead of splendid—the dependable part
of the garden.

The shoot is shrimpy, yes, but something fleshy
around the stem, like a cub paw—a clue to the
size of the roar ahead, and sure enough by June,
the thing is cattail high, thick stalked with new
leaves curling open each day, sudden as tongues.
By July climbs up to the fence ledge, commencing—
steady and serenely territorial—its full assault
toward the oregano.

It's taking over, I say. *It's going to flower,*
you say, poking at knobs swelling the top of
the stalk, and just like that all August long,
while deficits rise and prospects fall, while
madmen with Uzis are loose in our corridors,
and people in places with unpronounceable names
murder each other in unspeakable ways,

while our friends stop divorcing and start
dying and our kids begin leading their own
imperfect lives—all August long, that damned
thing detonates into flower, discharging one
by one its yellow flares as if our lives
depended on it.

WEDDING DAY

I
The day plays down to waiting:
my dress, ready, drapes the closet door—
the mothers are wearing burgundy tonight—
my suede shoes, burgundy, below,
toe in to the rim of the rug.

All afternoon, snow
piles down the December sky,
gathers to a white wool on the window
ledge, as all the days gather
to this all but last one of the year,
your wedding day,

II
A sudden flutter at the door
and you standing there—
your face painfully open,
with your new haircut
and your thumbnail
to be fixed,

that old action
between us, easy—
easy at the first:
sleek skin insulted at
knee, finger, elbow,
Tonka truck, wounded
at the wheel.

That old action between us:
the Mercurochrome,
the cookie, the kiss,
the fix no longer mine
to give.

Still, your long thumb
steady in my left hand,
scissors lifted in my right—
I pare away the offending
crescent, even out
the edge.

III
If at the first
there was nothing to you
but wanting, small wonder
the habit of wanting for you
followed so soon after—
I settled as easy into it
as that old tartan lap robe,
the one big enough to cover
us both.

It is no small
comfort to me, then,
that the girl you got
is the girl you wanted,
the one you waited for,
the way your tux, tails,
patent wing tips wait in my
closet, patient, preening
for the first dance,

and as if today
you were finished with
waiting, finished with wanting,
I feel a stillness in your fingers,
the answering stillness
in mine.

SPOCK ADDENDUM

For Maura

The hard part is not
doing. That will come
easier than you know:
the first stipple of
milk, the meteor shower—
the bouncing, balancing,
rocking. All the troll
costumes, lemon bars,
birthday cakes—the
staying hand, the stilling
voice—I tell you

who do the doing part
so well, how ably you'll
oar the small craft of
each morning forward
through all the pools,
eddies, backwaters, past
shoals and quagmires,
lift and dip of your
paddle steady,
systolic.

The hard part is
not doing, a movement
downstream that may
look like drifting from
the far shore but has
nothing to do with
drifting. Not steering,
not saying either
but a way of responding
to the current under
you—a question of

balance, really—the
cells at full attention
to each surge, each
shallow, each ambient
breeze: a weight shift
here, a small adjustment
there. No matter the day
is glass, the visibility
splendid—you'll never
exactly know what lies
behind the next
turning.

Sit still. Listen.
Don't hold too tight.
It will be the best,
the wildest, ride
you'll ever have.

SACRED PRECINCT

What a language it is, the laughter of women,
high-flying and subversive.
Long before law and scripture
we heard the laughter, we understood freedom.

—**LISEL MUELLER**
  from "The Laughter of Women"

TO THE WOMAN WHO WILL OPEN THIS TIME CAPSULE 100 YEARS FROM NOW

I am sending you the Sonia Henie doll
on miniature skates—
everything to be desired, balanced
on the edges of serrated blades.

I am sending you the waist cincher
I wore to my first dance,
the Merry Widow I wore to my last—
breasts pressed up, out, together—
twin offerings on the altar.

I am sending you the hip smoother,
tummy-hugger hose, two-way
stretch, three-way mirror that hissed
every morning of my insufficiency,
and I am sending you my bridal veil
behind whose tulle I peered out
at a newly narrowed universe.

I am sending you the stories:
the one about the girl whose life
was a slumber till awakened
by the kiss of a prince,
and the one about the girl
whose life was servitude till
saved by the favor of a prince,

and I am sending you the Book
about the women in whose
ever-receptive, ever-waiting
wombs God played out His
holy plans for men.

I hope you will open
this package tenderly
as one might open the low
door of a forgotten playhouse,
all the while remembering
childhood—the pleasures, yes,
but also the gated-off rooms,
the hushes,
the harrowing dependencies.

I hope you will try to find
us here, hidden as we are,
among the shards of what
we thought we were.

TALK

We talk about Bosnia, Rwanda,
Los Angeles—the mystery of
Shlafly, the muzzling of Hillary,
between sips of decaf cappuccino,
always between sips, we talk:

about Peggy's elbow, Jorie's knee
about estrogen, cholesterol,
Doris's depression.
> *I swear I couldn't believe I was getting myself into*
> *the same old shit.*

> *I know*

We talk about men, those large,
skulking others we love, live with,
the ones we manage finally to leave,
the ones who summarily dump us.
We translate them into languages
we can understand, measure
the downside of transcendence.
> *So he was in his passive-aggressive mode and I know*
> *what I was feeling. Intimidated.*

> *I know*

We talk about our kids, those least
protectable pieces of ourselves
out flailing about in the bang
and buffet of the general joy—
play yard, school yard, bingo!
the botched interviews, the blighted
love affairs, and how next time,
we will know how not to know their pain.

>   *And the worst part was I heard my mother's words*
>   *coming out of my own mouth.*

>   *I know*

We stir the foam down into
the coffee, sprinkle with a little
more chocolate...*I know, I know*

>   *I know*

CHERRY PIE*

What can I tell you, she had nothing. Nothing
from the start. The fourth girl and welcome
as the plague

> *Why KILL a child due to fear?*

    Line 9-inch
    pie plate
    with

    pastry, roll
    out bottom
    crust.

so when he asks her to marry him, what did she have
to lose? Begged her and wept, which told her pretty quick the kind of
man
he was.   A zero.

> *Some women LOVE women*
> *1. Better sex*
> *2. Doubles your wardrobe*

    Combine
    tapioca
    sugar, cherries,
    almond
    extract, and butter.

Oh, I knew what it was,
all right, the dark

stain in my pants. Hey Mom!
I yelled, I've got the
Curse!

> *Does anyone think they're*
>   *perfect? I FEEL like I am*

And when he came
over that afternoon,
my folks out, I'd
already figured this
would be the day

there on my bed
in the middle
of a Monday

I wasn't ready to be a MOTHER
so I gave my baby to someone else

Let stand
fifteen minutes

Zero about the best she could expect and when
he started running out on her, believe me, he gave her the world to see.
Let's
face it. What a man can't get at home, he looks around for.

I THINK probably war is
testosterone poisoning,
slavery too.

Well, she says looking
hard at me like it was the
first thing I'd done in my

whole life. Mazel Tov, she
says, and spanks my bottom
three times. For good luck.

Adjust top
crust. Turn
into lined
pie plate.

I was 18 and pregnant too with NO
husband.

In the middle of a
Monday, like, what the
hell. Later I walked him

to the subway,
strangely weightless
like finals over—
summer break about to begin

> Bake till
> filling is tender and
> crust is browned.

She moved him to the spare room. Never
slept with him again. Leave him? Go? Where would she go? She had the
house. She was happy. A worm wakes up in horseradish, he thinks it's
cherry pie.

Are you brain dead?
Then it's time to WAKE UP

> Especially
> nice
> served warm.

---

* With special thanks to the young women who talk to each other on the walls of
the W.C., Harlan Center, College of Marin.

HIKING WITH HELEN

We start, of course, from her house
and while she's busy pulling on her boots,
I address the treasures at the tall oak table—
whims she's set aside for me since last time:
a *Far Side* from the Sunday paper,
a snapshot, maybe,
with an earlier Helen, flanked by cousins,
smiling into the thin sun of another spring,
or maybe, in late summer, the first fruits
of her pear tree.

Then walking out into the latticed light
of a Mill Valley morning,
our pace becomes a conversation,
our conversation a way of traveling:
talking becomes a kind of listening
listening a kind of talking
when I'm hiking with Helen.

And by the time we lean into the climb,
we start to shed the shawls, sweats,
flannel shirts—
layers no longer relevant—
so that climbing becomes a way
of discarding what we do not need.

And if, on the hilltop,
Helen spreads her arms wide
to the wild lilac, the lupine, the levels
of meadow descending from green to green,
and yells, to no one in particular,

                              Thank you!

I'll be sure to add *Amen.*

SACRED PRECINCT

For my granddaughter

Then went up Moses, and Aaron, Nadab, and Abihu,
and seventy of the Elders of Israel: and they saw the
God of Israel…and did eat and drink.

—EXODUS 24:9–11

They are men, the Elders—
you can count on it, dear.
For one thing, God doesn't
much talk to women (Hagar,
yes, but only to save her son).
No, He doesn't exhort or wrestle
with women at all, and after Eden,
doesn't much trust us either.

And for another—the matter
of eating and drinking. While
the Elders gazed upon the Blessed
Face (time sliding away to a stop,
the ground below their lives
suffused to a blue glow),
someone needed to be at the fire,
turning a roast, steadying a kettle.

I see them there, the women at
Sinai, in the molten light of desert
dusk, much as I remember your
great-great-grandmother
and her daughters preparing
the seder meal each spring,
faces flushed from the fire,
hair caught back with kerchiefs,
laughter rising from the stew pots
like a sabbath prayer—the air inside
the room heady with the pleasure
of their mutual affections.

I see them there, together,
in the sacred precinct
of each other's company—
Grandma setting up the bowls,
Jennie checking out the progress
of the men's transactions with
the Blessed Name. *Quick!*
she cries, eyes lit with divine
intent, *Quick, they're already*
up to the fourth blessing.
It's time to pour the soup!

SARAH

Each month, the terrible
blood, skull of a moon
gaping to a barren sky.
What could it matter to
me, the covenant they
cooked between them on
the sizzling plain of
Moreh—he and his God
negotiating the limits
of land, obligation, the
projected revenues of my
womb, while the Egyptian
whore lorded it over me,
her belly swelling before
my eyes—a great pustule
rising from the center of
my pain. What do I care
for Canaan or a Void that
does not choose to speak
to me? What would I want
with a nation, needing
only the kingdom of
a single baby's touch?

This time, the voice lit in his ear
familiar as a housefly. *Lord, here I am,*
he answered, flicking at the lobe absently—
he was old now, his moves more tentative—

his hearing not what it was in Ur
when a single syllable could catapult
him blind toward Canaan.
The boy ran before him in pursuit

of the phantom lamb, hair bouncing
with each footfall, burnished, in
the high mountain light. So even
had he heard the message right,

he knew at once, in a deep shudder of
love (the boy turning to him open-faced,
dark eyes wide, unshadowed)
that what was asked he could not do.

For even had he heart for it, there was
the woman, who, in old age, had nurtured
all the world in her long barren womb.
No, he said softly. *No.*

Better my lands and all of Canaan
cancelled, better the blessed covenant
torched, no, better my worthless life
cut off now, here, Lord—than raise

my hand against my own
or anybody's son! Then God looked
down into the upturned mirror of
the man's face, and at long last

recognized His own.
It had taken 5,000 years—an eyelid's
flicker and no time at all for God.
And He looked down on the waters

and the dry land Earth, at whales,
cattle, and all the creeping things.
He looked down on Abraham, Sarah,
and Isaac—on Hagar and Ishmael,

and God saw that it was good.
And the evening and the morning
was the first day.

LEAH

Imagine this: You are two
months shy of nineteen
and it is your own father
who veils you, leads you
under veil of darkness
to the man's bed.

You have not yet learned to resist,
but when he takes you at once in
the darkness there, all the while braying
your sister's name, something in you
clenches forever against him—a resistance
of nipples, knees, pudenda—
witness to what your body could bear.

You bear him sons in spite,
suckle all four on the thin milk
of spite, from which they draw
such sustenance as they require
to spite her braying son.

Now in the last light of evenings,
he likes to tell you stories of his God,
how Evil came into the world with a woman
and a snake. Fool! who robbed his brother
of his birthright and you of every sweetness
you might otherwise have known.

Evil, you tell him, has nothing to do
with apples. Look how the First Murder
was an act of the unloved son.

Evil, you tell him, is a natural
action, the best and last recourse
of the Unchosen. Tell your God, you
tell him, if He would tweeze out
Evil from the human heart, He must first
pluck away Favor—that tragic faculty
to choose and unchoose.

Haven't you lain awake each night
these thirty years, feeling the cold steel
of his indifference twist deeper, ever
deeper into your life? Haven't you drawn each
waking breath thinking how best to turn
the tip back into his own fool heart?

LOT'S WIFE

Hurry! he hissed through his teeth,
Hurry! all morning as I loaded
my life onto three handcarts. *Can't
you smell it,* he bawled, *the place
stinks of sinning! Sinning,* he said,
who only last night offered our
daughters up like just-picked figs
to two hollow-eyed strangers. Only
an animal doesn't look back. How
can I know where I'm going without
knowing where I've been? I turned
to see the sweet curve of the hill
above my home—my mother, arm
still raised, grown small—pale as
a moth in the glitter of the noon
sky. Then nothing.   Salt.   Of tears
sweat   semen.   Only an animal
has no name. My mother named me
Zachora. It means Remember.

AND FINALLY, AMELIA TELLS IT TO THE PRESS

Suppose you'd grown
beyond compassion,
beyond the sudden tweak
of need, the tug of
human love.

Suppose the traps were
sprung, the categories
that contained you
emptied:
wife   daughter
helpmate   nurse
the small rooms where
you'd played your life
in hushed half tones—

why then a plane
becomes your music,
the instrument panel
spread out before you
like a keyboard only
you know how to play.

Why talk to me of loss?
I held the whole sky
in my right hand—
warm body of the throttle
quivering in my fingers
like a finch—

drew the long stick
downward to my knee,
then rose oh slowly
through the slanted air
toward daybreak.

ELEVEN

For Arlene

She is eleven in the forefront
of the photograph, horizon
of cousins on the beach behind her,
a sister on either side—
the younger, rapt in the particular
oblivion of sand castles,
the older, with the new camera
smile tentatively attached,
shoulders hunched inward
over the new breasts.

But she is eleven, cross-legged,
head high, smile wide,
uncompromised.
Look at me, it says, and she is
something, all right, centered
as she is on all the balance
beams between the school yard
and her storybooks.

It will be forty years before
the world will hold so steady,
so still again beneath her feet.
Meanwhile, biology will begin
its hormonal high step, spin her
once, twice, nine times around
the room, utterly up-end her.

Meanwhile, the chorus of voices
will reshape her—tighten her
belly, her thighs, her smile.
She will learn to lower her gaze.

She will not recognize
her face until a day years
later on an opposite shore,
when kneeling in the sand,
camera cocked, she cries,
Here! Look here a minute!
And her granddaughter
turns to her and smiles.

USED BOOK

To Piggy from
Gipsy
This 28th of November '54

The Flemish text succumbs
to color plates by page 18—
the subject being Leonardo,
not a moment too soon,
for here is the *Virgin of*
the Rocks, at rest in her
grotto, face draped in light,
the angel of *Annunciation,*
wings detailed for immediate
takeoff, all the anatomical
studies of muscle bunches,
viscera, and bone,

and in the center, wedged
between the *Mona Lisa*
and *Cecilia Gallerani,*
a photograph,

a portrait, studio posed,
of a lovely young woman,
head canted to one side,
eyebrows arched, fair hair
folded into the pageboy
of the day, just brushing her
bare shoulders—and rising
from the shadow space
behind her, the single word
"Remember?"

It seems unlikely whoever
filed the photo between
these pages would not.
Or was the Gipsy of
the inscription another
lovely girl entirely?
And who was this lover
of women and Leonardo?
Someone, perhaps, like
the Zoharist, who situated
Beauty at the very center
of the tree of life,
someone who knew where
things belong.

REVELATION

For every exile who walked out
of Egypt between walls of water,
for everyone who remembered
the feel of sea bottom underfoot,
the sibilant roar of water rearing
on the right, on the left, someone
forgot. Someone scanning

the dry horizon for a well,
or already mourning the musky
smell of autumn in her father's
fig trees, forgot the hosannahs,
and, by the bitter waters of Marah,
forgot the flash of dancing feet,
the shimmer of timbrels.

For every proselyte at Sinai,
someone never heard the horns
at all. Someone turned back from
the mountain to bank the fire,
feed the baby, steal a secret
moment with another.

Revelation begins in attention:
While the elders trembled before
the word of God flowing down
the scorched north flank of Sinai,
someone, rising from a last long
embrace, gazed into the rapt face
of the beloved and saw
that it was good.

AMNESTY LETTERS

What fortitude the Soul contains
That it can so endure
The accent of a coming Foot—
The opening of a door—

—**EMILY DICKINSON**
from Poem No. 1760

THE DEAD

Just as you'd hoped, they
are sitting on folding chairs
in Jennie's backyard. It's
always autumn there, late-
afternoon light splicing
across asphalt, talk
unfocused, desultory, for
there's all the time in

the world—time to decide
who'll stay for dinner, who
needs to pick up a pack of
cigarettes, who'll start
washing the lettuce—
just as there's nowhere
really to go: They cross
and uncross legs,
shift leisurely on slatted

seats while Moey goes
in to check the Dodger
game. It's always two
and two with a man on,
right in the middle of
the inning and the score
is always what it is. So
there's no pain here, not
because the talk is
more solicitous,

the strudel sweeter,
but because no one ever
leaves. In fact, no one
moves much, only Jennie,
who in perpetuity appears

and reappears, bearing
jelly-centered lemon drops,
tea in *yahrzeit* glasses,
flames still simmering
through beveled

edges. *Steady that*
tray! they cry, *Sit down*
already! The woman's
killing herself! and having
thought of it so aptly, they
slap their thighs and die
laughing.

THE DREAM

This time, Mama,
we meet in the shopping mall.
The roof's glassed over now,
but there we are in the old place,
wind busy between the buildings,
and you look as you always look
in my dreams, distracted, somehow,
and dying,

so inquiring how you are
seems specious, but I ask it
anyway, as always, and this time,
with that sudden shrug of eyebrows
you have something to tell:

Let's face it, you say, leaning toward me,
your voice all conspiracy, *I have no appetite.*

How I lose you then I can't remember,
but all night long I race
past sale racks at Magnin's, past
Cal's Camera and the old cafeteria,
the people at the steam tables
diving at their food
like dolphins.

All night long I race
past plate-glass windows,
looking for you.

GLASS

You enter this space
through a storefront, window
emblazoned for the all the world
to see: MAX STRAUS, GLASS—

on this night, shades drawn
down against the bladed eyes
of strangers. Inside, the seder
table runs lengthwise down

the room, balanced between
ceiling-high racks of glass
sheets shelved end to end,
green edges glistening. On

all other nights, he'd be
just now shuffling through
the door, settling his handcart
of mirrors and windows to

rest, but on this night,
already in place at the head
of his table, flanked by uncles,
he commences the mysterious

guttural drone, pausing only
to perform such miracles as
the text requires. All of
your life when you think of

him, you think of him like
this: blue crystal flicker of eyes
between high, wide cheekbones,
gnarled forefinger touching

once each: egg, bitter herbs,
shank bone, matzoh—*Behold
the bread of our affliction*—
dipping one at a time, from

out of his kiddush cup, ten
plagues, each a bead of red
wine on a milk-glass plate.

WINTER IN THE PHOTOGRAPH

It is winter in the photograph, the way
only old black-and-whites can convey
such city cold—you wear the kind
of overcoat they used to bundle
little boys in those winters—buttoned
to the throat, cut just above the knee.

Hair just slicked to one side, you are
seated on the school steps, not yet
three, three small stones beside you—
gravel on gravel—dark eyes wide,
defiant, gazing straight at the photographer,
long upper lip set firm against the lower

in a straight line set against
the something raging softly about you.

Sweetheart, I want to say, the world is good.
I am coming tomorrow with chocolate Mallomars,
the blue Schwinn with balloon tires,
and a father.

Only—how would I know you, then, when
we meet twenty years from now, under
the eaves of the office porch? Whose
eyes, uncircumcized by sorrow, would
question mine that July, beside the lake,
our faces fired with shadow?

SIDNEY

Blue skies, smilin' at me
Nothing but blue skies
Do I see.

When you left for work that morning
in October, the Persian lambs in hock
to pay the minks, the minks in hock
to pay the rent, the rent in hock to
pay the interest, when you left her with
a kiss and a box of birthday bittersweets,
the space you left was vast, sudden—
as if the seven-story house next door
had vanished in the night, the light
at her window profoundly altered.

First she waited, set another pot
of coffee up to boil, some cocoa for
the boy—eye fixed to the little slit
of light at the door, ear narrowed to
a sputter of key, then she called:
the brother who was looking for you too,
the mother who cried they'd been undone,
the police who told her about easy loans
from hard people. Then she waited.

When you disappeared into the
Depression, a song on your lips,
did you just keep going—head west,
your debt receding in the eastern sky
like a flock of ragged wings? Did you get
yourself another gentle-willed wife,
another spittin' image son? No, not

you! They would have had to put a bullet
through your head to hold you off from
home—weight your carcass with a rock,
drop you to the bottom of the East River,
close your mouth with stone, Sidney.
How otherwise this silence, this dirge
of fierce indifference you've sung
for sixty years?

PARADISE

He is waiting for her.

After the long withdrawal
of her last breath
he is there
as she saw him last
in his gray fedora
and overcoat, box
of Barracini chocolates
in his hand.

Look at you, he cries,
Where have you been?
I've been waiting forever!

Waiting, she says, smoothing
a few white wisps behind her
ear, unhappy with the cut
of her hospital gown,
I've been waiting
seventy years. Alone.
What could I think but
you'd run out on me?

Never, he says, eyes
darkening. *Didn't you know*
only death could part us?

Then he opens the brocade
box, chooses from the center
one chocolate-covered cherry,
her favorite, and holds it
to her lips.

She had not eaten in weeks,
had sworn off chocolate
years before, but at the first
bite, the bitter undertaste
of her long life melted off
in an instant, like snow
before the first blaze of April,

and just like that, she entered
the paradise she'd always
known could not exist,
especially not for her.

THE SCAR

grows
inward now, domestic,
traces meticulously
the breast curve under
the arm in tentative
pencil stroke, only
the ledge of swelling
below remembers needle
prick, stitch, scalpel—
the deep assault to
the flesh.

That's me
that's where
I've been, he says
smiling, fingering
the seam, knot incised,
sutures slipped free.
You're one lucky
girl, he says.

Mustache
fluttering, he moves
among his gleaming
rooms, among his
patients in their
paper jerkins perched
like timorous birds
on the edges of
examining tables

and
one Wednesday
morning, peels
back the skin flap,
subtracts the innocuous
node, restores to you
intact your one lucky
life.

The scar
grows usual now,
even the terror that
feasted all week inside
your ribs is gone, the
panic that dogged you
banished

down
to where the
one fear, sprawled
in its dark metastases
waits patient,
voracious.

ASHES

Again we are initialing
our living wills, revisiting
our pledges to murder each
other when the machines
render us machines. Again
we consider the matter of
ashes, and despite your
gloomy certainties about
finality, I know otherwise.

At sea, you say, and I can
see you winching in the halyard,
letting out the main, spirit
filling with a good beam
breeze to carry you out
the Gate toward open sea,
where everything sloughs
away but wind and water.

But I opt for shore—
swells, spray, urchins
lurking on the slimy
bottom, never were my element—
fine enough for a langorous
day adrift, but for
eternity? No, I choose
earth, air—any place
inklings of green emerge

toward light. How, out
of sight of land, would I
know when spring begins?
I opt for some hilltop at
the water's edge, where I
can listen all day to
the long wheeze of the sea,
watch at evening for when
you're coming home.

MATTERS OF SURVIVAL

Regarding matters of survival. It's been established
that the flesh, threatened, feeds on its own muscle.

Which may explain how since you died I've managed
on a Valium a day, and the easy succor of outrage:

Thief! twice you took my future.
First when they laid you on my belly in the birth room
and I knew the weight of you against my life.
Next when they laid you in the earth and I knew
the ark was empty, the covenant cancelled.

Liar! You told me youth would be your amulet
against infection. You told me you'd grown
trail-shrewd on the Sherpa paths and immune
to darkness, rising to the last long shards
of moonlight on the peaks of Sagarmatha.

You told me you'd be coming home next August.

AMNESTY LETTERS

Excellency, I am writing to you from
the still of my kitchen from the death
of a dream I fought all night to forget,
regarding the matter of Artyom Badzhgovich
Dzhopua, who, it appears, was "disappeared"
from Dranda Prison some time ago and whose
whereabouts, this shimmerimg morning, remain
unknown, knowing that if nothing can be lost in
God's eye—not even Artyom—then something
might be found in Georgia, in Abkhazia, in
your good graces.   Even Artyom.

Dr. President, as for Marta Maria Vega
Cabrera, who in the Western Women's Prison
has been attacked by prisoners and prison
guards, I beg you to remember the terrible
zeal of your own youth: the hills, the hurried
camps, the immaculate guns. Dear Doctor, I
have a granddaughter now, whose eyes are
the color of amethyst, for whom I plead
the fate of Marta Maria. If zeal, as in
Marta's case, is what the soul grows on, then
evil, as in your case, is zeal metastasized.

Minister, Premier, Potentate, I am writing
to you from the trolley car, passengers
swaying strapped above me, while I doze
in a kind of darkness my life has never
allowed. I am writing on behalf of Jigme Sangpo,
Josephine Ngengi, Teresa Akumi, that they
not be forgotten. I am writing on behalf
of José Encarnación Barrera Orozco. I am
writing to you by the light of the open
eye of the TV whose gaze raises questions
I fail, always, to answer.

LOST

First off, the Birkenstocks that quick-stepped
up the morning side of Sinai, so well molded to
my soles, only to disappear along with one giant
tube of Coppertone and a room key by the shore

of a long-unparted Red Sea; a salmon-striped
shirt, quite vanished on the fourteenth floor of
what used to be the Broadway Sheraton; ditto
the traveling douche draped over a bath rod in

Llandudno; and twenty-eight pages of my manuscript,
bristling with metaphor, burned mistakenly (?)
along with the holiday mail; a very smiling
Sally Flynn, lips glistening with Cherries

in the Snow, in the red velvet she wore that
night of the freshman dance, before she was
banished into pregnancy and, being 1953,
oblivion—my own virginity not long after

on a gray December afternoon, lost less to
passion than the nuisance factor; three, maybe
four unborn babies of indeterminate sex whose
voiceless wails continue to wake me at 4 A.M.;

and two parents, consigned so long ago to my
private vision of the family plot line as to
be profoundly lost, except maybe Mama, once
again reminding me what would happen if my

head were not firmly affixed to my shoulders.

OUT THERE

What childishness is it that while there's a breath of life
in our bodies, we are determined to rush
to see the sun the other way around?

—ELIZABETH BISHOP
from "Questions of Travel"

WHEELS

The window seat please
and a morning so translucent,
hills up ahead turn to clock
glass.   You drive.   I'll
cradle my coffee in a
Styrofoam cup, strong, black
as licorice, a lust on my
tongue now in these hours
before we stop for breakfast.

I want to sip it really slow,
left foot curled up under me,
right resting on the dash.
I want to talk.   About
something: you   me   ours.
About nothing: whales
love   sunburn   semiotics
death.   I want
not to talk at all, turn

up the radio so the music
beats time to the tires,
settle back into leather-
smelling seats and watch
the world mile by from this
side of the windshield.
There's no place else to
be.   Wings   *cirio*
space   cactus   Catavina
stream   palm,   I want
to write this poem.

ALASKA

Cold.   Yes!   A glacier
makes its own season, and
long before we enter the Sound,
we feel it as a sudden withdrawal
of warmth, an unfriendly edge
to the air.

And out of scale, somehow.
Once seen, even the sea is
diminished by it, the great
black hills trivial in their
plunge to the water.

A tide of ice below the peak.
A white highway sliding down
the long slope seaward.
Surely this is what
we've come to see:

the blue-spattered crevasses,
the great blocks of ice wall
falling free, breaking forward—
all hush and thunder, the small
gray seals lolling about us on
ice floes like angels
too sated to fly.

If there are things
we'd better never know,
places we were never meant
to see, this may be one. It
will be at least a mountain and
a prairie east, two weeks,
four rivers and six cities

south, before that ice
begins retreating
from our rooms, our
dreams, our fingers.

THE DAY WE SAW THE ELEPHANT

the road was dusty along the high plain,
the driver leading us in a silent
choreography—rolling, unrolling windows
as trucks rose, fell behind us in brown

billows. The air was heavy in the back
seat. Heat, fatigue, the hundred nattering
irritations of the long-married, hung
over between us like mosquito netting,

smothering any inclination toward
talk. We must have dozed after
the last village, then jolted awake,
stopped suddenly in a forest

of acacia, the driver intoning: *Look,*
look here! And there he was before us:
a bull, not fully grown, tusks just
brushing the lower branches, ears fanned

out like two great sails, filling,
emptying the afternoon breeze. Holding
us a moment in his heavy-lidded gaze,
he paused, then continued teeing up

the new grass in a gesture elegant
as a soft-shoe—small flick of the left
foot, tip up from trunk to hidden
grin, and I loved you again there

in an instant, and the afternoon was
a sudden lace of light in the acacia.

THE RENDEZVOUS CAFE

There were three tables,
two stools at the counter,
a cook named Tom Kinnon
and no customers but us.

Pea soup, "Spicy Chicken,"
and in between,
Tom Kinnon talking
of cane crops and floods
up toward Tully River.

There was a menu on one wall,
a map of the world on the other—
but in reverse though, the world,
some kind of local joke,

Australia floating up top
like a seaborne tea tray,
Alaska fallen sodden
to the bottom,

home all but hidden
under that awful weight
of equator.

Where are we? we echoed,
fingers sweeping over oceans
feeling out familiar chinks
in the flanks of continents.

Later, Tom
walked us to our car,
the night air feral
with sea smells.

Here, he said,
one arm stretched
across my shoulders,
the other measuring out
the Milky Way,

sliding down under
to touch the diamond
of light, the four low stars
of the Southern Cross.
We're here.

BAHÍA DE BALLENAS

Slap of gray water at the side
of the hull, smells of sea, gasoline,
the outboard idling down
to a soft staccato.
Tail! Tail!, he cries, swinging
the tiller across his knees,
At one o'clock, Señora!
The great gray fan opens before us,
balances a moment, plunges below.
Gray skies part for a single shaft
of sunlight.
Twice more she comes, Señora!
Mira! Mira!
Top of the water turns slick.
Broad back glistening in a fine
frost of barnacles, she floats
alongside the way the dark shape of
a dream can float alongside you
all morning long, then disappear.
But first she breathes
(ten suns shimmer in the ripples of her fins)
and we alongside her breathe,
sharing the pleasure of air.

THE ROTHORN

Some mountains
are like this: the morning
dark, the start
tentative—

you pass quickly
through cows on lower
slopes, their faces floating
like lanterns above the grass,
bells lowing, and begin to
bend into the hard
part of the
climb

when what
has passed for
conversation dies—
the art required for it
factored out, as it must be
at the end, when breath
becomes the only
measure.

Some peaks
are so barren, lacking
bees or easy foothold,
so cloud-baffled, shrouded
by lesser, lovelier mountains,
so hidden you do not
see them till the last
and then you can't remember
why you came, nothing at all
remaining

but the crunch
of feet ahead, scree
fields failing away on
either edge, breath reaching
down into the center of your
life. You climb past desire
to the rocky
top,

your moment of
triumph, if any,
truncated, surely,
knowing the way
down will be
harder.

THE FALLING

Bottom of the great granite
bowl racing toward me,
pale avalanche of sky, rock,
tops of pine below—

and all the while thinking
it   is   happening
it is happening to me.

Weeks after, I return to it—
the moment the slow
measured move turned into
a slide, the inched sitting

my way downslope gained
momentum—Cathedral Peaks
behind me, Tenaya Lake
a cat's eye glitter below—

return to the exact
precipitous instant my
purchase on the universe
turned slick, and I watched

my life slide soles first
down the long stone sill.
I don't believe I screamed
or it would be there still—

a single small note spiraling
in the wide, incisive spaces
between peaks. I can't say
I saw my life slide by—in

that blue skidding instant
there was no space for past
or future, no space for
terror, only the glint of

water in rock hollows,
granite rasping the backs
of my thighs, only the
falling, and with it, like

the time Bobby Sandler kissed
me in the sixth-grade wardrobe,
silence,
a suspension of all breath

my lips rounded in a single
syllable of surprise.

EDGES OF THE UNIVERSE

In the instant
after the first flame
licks—low hiss of
fire, blue ash
of bone—

the instant
before my mineral
soul spins out past
polar snow, moon stone,
shedding gravity and
all its vegetable
imperatives,

past the voice
in the whirlwind
and the whirlwind,

past Aleph and the
black holes, loss
of love, past
love—

I wake once
more to trolley
bells on Coney
Island Avenue,
knowing in the
night—as you do
somehow—there's
a lot more night
to go,

the door open
to a narrow shaft
of light, funneled
down the long
hall from the
living room,

and under the
rumble of radio—
voices—their voices,
blurred, blending,
holding down the
edges.

OUT THERE

Inside the circuits of the brainpan,
fuses light up like pinball bulbs
creating a world each moment
out of smoke and synapses.
All I see is all I *can* see, just as
this housefly, paused fitful beside me
on the sofa pillow, projects me forth
in multiple on the lenses of
an eight-sided eye.

Still, the redwood branches brushing
my window are out there, all right,
however altered, squeezed
through all the narrow alleys
of my mind, as are the chalk
angles of the city opposite,
suspended somewhere between
sky and water, as is Paris out there,
certainly, in whatever form it comes:
translated, temporary, ravishing.

Notes

The epigraph for the section page "First Time" is excerpted from "Burnt Norton" from *Four Quartets* by T. S. Eliot, copyright © 1936 by Harcourt, Inc., and renewed 1964 by T. S. Eliot. Reprinted by permission of the publisher.

The epigraph for the section page "The House" is by William Carlos Williams, from *Collected Poems: 1909–1939, Volume 1,* copyright © 1938 by New Directions Publishing Corp. Reprinted by permission of New Directions Publishing Corp.

The epigraph for the section page "Sacred Precinct" is reprinted by permission of Louisiana State University Press from *Alive Together: New and Selected Poems,* by Lisel Mueller. Copyright © 1996 by Lisel Mueller.

The epigraph for the section page "Amnesty Letters" is reprinted by permission of the publishers and the Trustees of Amherst College from *The Poems Of Emily Dickinson,* Thomas H. Johnson, ed., Cambridge, Mass: The Belknap Press of Harvard University Press, copyright © 1951, 1955, 1979 by the President and Fellows of Harvard College.

The epigraph for the section page "Out There" is an excerpt from "Questions of Travel" from *The Complete Poems: 1927–1979* by Elizabeth Bishop. Copyright © 1979, 1983 by Alice Helen Methfessel. Reprinted by permission of Farrar, Straus and Giroux, LLC.

Jacqueline Kudler lives in Sausalito, California, and teaches classes in writing and literature at the College of Marin, Kentfield. Her poems have appeared in numerous literary reviews and anthologies. An avid hiker, she published *Walking from Inn to Inn* (East Woods Press) in 1986, and co-writes a local hiking column for the *Pacific Sun* newspaper. *Sacred Precinct* is her first full collection of poems.

Sixteen Rivers Press is a shared-work, not-for-profit poetry collective dedicated to providing an alternative publishing avenue for San Francisco Bay Area poets. Founded in 1999 by seven women writers, the press is named for the sixteen rivers that flow into San Francisco Bay.

Also from Sixteen Rivers Press:

difficult news, by Valerie Berry
Translations from the Human Language, by Terry Ehret
Snake at the Wrist, by Margaret Kaufman
What I Stole, by Diane Lutovich
After Cocteau, by Carolyn Miller

San Joaquin * Fresno * Chowchilla * Merced * Tuolumne * Stanislaus * Calaveras * Bear
Mokelumne * Cosumnes * American * Yuba * Feather * Sacramento * Napa * Petaluma